# MY RIDING BOOK

For the _____ season.
**YEAR**

**HarperFestival**

*A Division of* HarperCollins*Publishers*

# My Name is _____

PLACE A PHOTO OF YOU AND YOUR PONY HERE

I'm ____ years old and I started riding when I was ____. I started riding because _____

_____. I usually ride ____ times a week.

**My instructor(s) is (are)** _____

**When I compete, I ride for** *(name of club or stable; if you are riding independently, you can say "myself"!)* _____

_____

**My riding buddies are** _____

**What I like most about riding is** _____

**My pony's<sup>∪</sup> show name is**_____
*(If he doesn't have one, what name would you make up for him?)*

**His stable name is**_____

**He is a**_____**-year-old** *(color and breed)* _____

**who stands**_____**hands tall. His special markings include**

_____

**The things I like best about my pony are**_____

_____

**Some of my pony's most interesting habits are**_____

_____

**My pony likes it when I**_____

_____

**If my pony could talk, I think he would sound like**_____

*HELPFUL HINT*

### SAFETY

Ponies can be timid animals that react quickly when frightened. Therefore, always speak to the pony when you walk up behind him and let him know you are there. When working around him, stay close so that you are less likely to be hit if he kicks.

∪ *To keep things simple, we're going to say "pony" even though you may be riding a horse, and we will call your pony a "he" even though you may be riding a mare.*

# My Stable

PLACE A PHOTO OF YOUR STABLE HERE

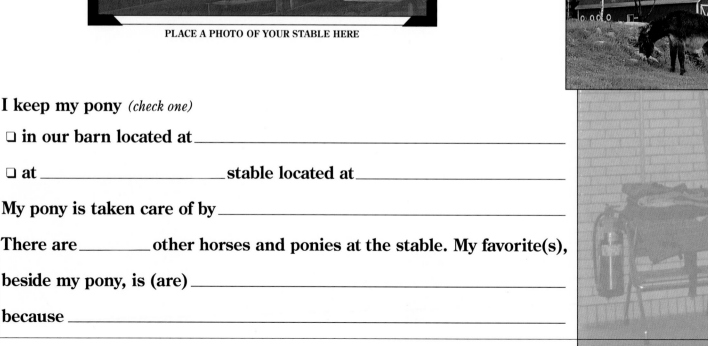

**I keep my pony** *(check one)*

❑ **in our barn located at** _____

❑ **at** _____ **stable located at** _____

**My pony is taken care of by** _____

**There are** _____ **other horses and ponies at the stable. My favorite(s),**

**beside my pony, is (are)** _____

**because** _____

4

**If I could build my dream stable, it would look like this** *(Draw a picture of your dream stable, showing its overall shape, and, if you like, its floor plan. Be sure to show those special features you might like, such as a dressing room, a tack room, a VCR, an indoor arena, a soda machine, a game room, and so on)*:

**STABLE SAFETY**

Safe barns and stables always include a working fire extinguisher, buckets, hoses, running water, and more than one exit for ponies and people. Feed and potentially dangerous tools such as pitchforks and shovels should be stored away from ponies.

HELPFUL HINT

What seems to relax my pony most when he is in his stall is _____

_____

Some of the barn animals at my pony's stable are *(list kinds and names)*: _____

_____

Some of the funniest things barn animals do are _____

_____

⑤

# How I Feed My Pony

My pony eats _____ times a day.

**This is his daily feed schedule**
*(include the times of day he is usually fed, and how
much and what kinds of feed and/or hay he gets)*: _____

_____

_____

_____

_____

**When my pony eats, he sounds like** _____

_____

**His favorite treats are** _____

_____

**I give him these when** _____

_____

**SNACKS**

HELPFUL HINT

An occasional treat for your pony is fine, but don't overdo it. Frequent treat giving can spoil your pony, making him greedy, and too much of a good thing can make him sick.

**Q. What is colic and how can it be avoided?**

A. Colic is a stomach ailment in horses and ponies that can be caused by overeating, bad feed, working too soon after eating, or worms. The best way to prevent colic is to make sure your pony is properly cooled before feeding or watering, use a good quality feed and deworm him regularly. Signs of colic include restlessness, biting the flanks, sweating, and repeated lying down and getting up. At the first sign of colic, call the veterinarian and get your pony walking!

# How I Groom My Pony

The tools I use to groom my pony are _____

This is how I do the actual grooming: _____

_____

The most sensitive areas of my pony's body are _____

When I groom these areas I use _____

My best pony-grooming secrets are _____

_____

_____

# My Veterinarian

My vet's name is Dr. _____

The vet usually checks my pony *(when)* _____

_____

My pony gets shots to prevent the following diseases:

_____

_____

My pony is dewormed every _____ weeks.

Here's how: _____

The best medical advice I ever got for my pony was

_____

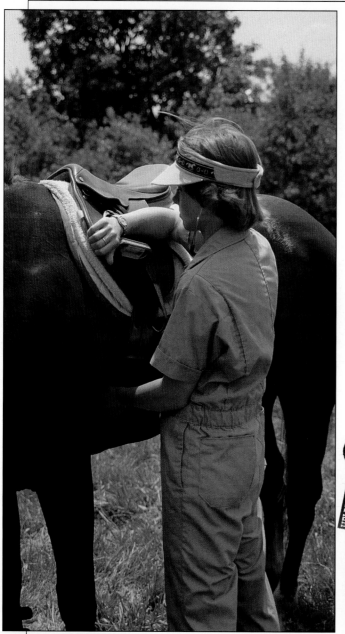

## HELPFUL HINT

## HEALTH

You can help prevent hoof problems in your pony by cleaning his hooves daily with a hoof pick. Never drop a hoof after cleaning it; always set it down gently.

VET CHECK

**Q. What is a pony's normal body temperature?**

A. 98–100.5° F. A temperature of 102° indicates a fever and any temperature over 104° should be considered high and reason to call the veterinarian.

# My Farrier

My farrier's name is _____

_____

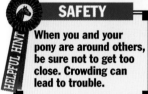

**SAFETY**

**HELPFUL HINT**

When you and your pony are around others, be sure not to get too close. Crowding can lead to trouble.

He/she usually comes to shoe or trim

my pony's hooves every_____weeks.

This is how the farrier does a shoeing
*(describe the steps in shoeing your pony)*:

_____

_____

_____

_____

TRACE ONE OF YOUR PONY'S HOOVES AND REDRAW IT HERE. INSIDE THE HOOF OUTLINE, DRAW AND LABEL THE PARTS. *(toe, quarter, heel, frog, wall, and sole)*

# My Pony's Tack

The tack that I normally use with my pony

Type of saddle and brand: _____

Type of girth: _____

Type of saddle pad: _____

Type of bit: _____

Type of bridle
*(how can you tell your bridle from the others in the barn?)*:

_____

Color and kind of halter: _____

I have these blankets for my pony
*(list and describe what you use them for)*:

_____

In addition, I use the following special gear:

_____

I clean my tack *(how often)* _____

This is how I do it: _____

_____

_____

**HELPFUL HINT!**

## TACK

Clean your bridle and girth after every session with your pony. Dirty tack can cause sores so never put it away dirty. As you clean tack, check for wear and tear, and never use any equipment that is unduly worn or broken. You should brush and dry out your saddle pad daily, launder it regularly, and wash your saddle with saddle soap before it begins to look dirty.

# Saddling and Bridling

I learned to saddle and bridle my pony when I was _____ years old.

When I bridle my pony, the trickiest part is _____

_____

The hardest part of saddling my pony is _____

_____

**Q. Why do riders mount their ponies from the left?**

• • • • • • • • • • • • • • • • • • • • • • • • • •

A. In the Middle Ages, knights wore their swords on the left, which made mounting their horses from the right impossible. The practice of mounting from the left continues to this day.

## TACKING UP

**HELPFUL HINT**

When putting a saddle on your pony's back, be sure it is far forward, close to the withers. After tightening the girth, pull the saddle pad up to the pommel so that air can circulate between your pony's spine and the pad.

# My Typical Riding Routine—
# Just My Pony and Me

My pony and I practice together_____times a week.

After tacking up my pony, I usually warm him up by

_____

I can tell he is warmed up when_____

_____

Then we begin our practice routine. A typical day's

practice usually includes these activities:_____

_____

Some things I like best about practicing with my pony are

_____

_____

The thing I like least about practicing with my pony is

_____

After we finish practicing, I usually do the following with

my pony: _____

_____

**I CAN TELL MY PONY'S MOOD FROM THESE BODY SIGNALS THAT HE GIVES:**

**1. HAPPY AND COMFORTABLE**

**2. ANGRY OR GROUCHY**

**3. FRIGHTENED**

**4. TIRED**

**5. FRISKY AND PLAYFUL**

**6. LOVING AND FRIENDLY**

**7. NOT INTERESTED IN SEEING ME**

**Q. When moving, how many natural rhythms can a pony have?**

A. Four. A pony's walk can be counted "1-2-3-4, 1-2-3-4..."; its trot can be counted "1-2, 1-2, 1-2, 1-2..."; its canter can be counted "1-2-3, 1-2-3, 1-2-3, 1-2-3..."; and its gallop is a quick "1-2-3-4, 1-2-3-4."

# Lessons with My Instructor

My instructor is _____. We work together____time(s) a week.

After warming my pony up, we usually start the lesson by

_____

Right now, my instructor has me working hardest on

_____

The things my instructor is ALWAYS telling me are

_____

What I like most about my lessons is _____

What I like least is _____

The scariest moment I ever had during a lesson was _____

The best moment was _____

The most important pieces of advice I have ever received
*(list one for each of the following areas)*:

Equitation, or form:_____

Jumping:_____

Safety:_____

Understanding how ponies think:_____

Thanks to what I have learned from my instructor, I can now do the following things with my pony *(check off your ability)*:

| SKILL | WELL | OK | NEED TO IMPROVE | CAN'T YET |
|---|---|---|---|---|
| WALK | | | | |
| CIRCLES | | | | |
| POSTING TROT | | | | |
| SITTING TROT | | | | |
| TROTTING POLES | | | | |
| CANTER | | | | |
| LOW JUMP | | | | |
| GALLOP | | | | |
| | | | | |
| | | | | |

My goals as I enter this show season are

_____

_____

# Memorable Days

Use this section to write about days with your pony that were especially memorable to you. Maybe you and your pony had a good lesson together, or a nice trail ride, or did something particularly fun together. What-ever the day was, tell why it was memorable to you, using your own thoughts and words.

**WHEN AND WHERE:**

✍

_____

_____

_____

_____

_____

**WHEN AND WHERE:**

✍

_____

_____

_____

_____

**WHEN AND WHERE:**

✍

_____

_____

_____

_____

**WHEN AND WHERE:**

✍️

**WHEN AND WHERE:**

✍️

# My Show Schedule

## This season I hope to enter these shows or competitions:

| SHOW | DATE |
|---|---|
| 1. | |
| 2. | |
| 3. | |
| 4. | |

| SHOW | DATE |
|---|---|
| 5. | |
| 6. | |
| 7. | |
| 8. | |

# My Preshow Routine

This is a list of things I do the day before I leave for a show:

_____

_____

_____

If I am trailering to the show, here is how I prepare my pony for the trip:

_____

If my pony could describe his feelings about trailering, he might say

_____

At the show itself, I keep busy before my first event by _____

_____

Some words that best describe my feelings at the start of a show are:

_____

**Q. Good pasture and fields always have four important elements. What are they?**

A. Lots of clean, fresh water Plenty of good grass Shelter and shade Safety — no bad fences, holes in field, sharp objects lying around, or barbed wire

---

### WHAT I PUT IN MY TACK BOX

JJF

- ❏ Saddle
- ❏ Girth
- ❏ Saddle pad
- ❏ Bridle
- ❏ Boots
- ❏ Helmet
- ❏ Gloves
- ❏ Jacket

- ❏ Hair net
- ❏ Riding crop
- ❏ Cooler
- ❏ Leg wraps
- ❏ Curry comb
- ❏ Brush
- ❏ Sponges
- ❏ Towels

- ❏ Sweat scraper
- ❏ Liniment
- ❏ Tool kit
- ❏ First aid kit
- ❏ Buckets
- ❏ Hoof dressing
- ❏ Hoof pick

**OTHER THINGS I PUT IN MY TACK BOX:**

- ❏ _____
- ❏ _____
- ❏ _____
- ❏ _____

## NAME OF SHOW                                    WEATHER

_____

## MY FIRST CLASS WAS

_____

### What my pony and I did best in this class was

_____

We finished _____

Warming up before my first class, I felt _____

_____

## A LATER CLASS WAS

_____

### When my number was called, I felt _____

_____

_____

### What my pony and I did best was _____

_____

### We finished _____

## MY LAST CLASS WAS

_____

### Going into the class I felt _____

_____

_____

### My best moment in this event was _____

_____

### My pony and I finished _____

**HELPFUL HINT**

**ARM POSITION**

Think of your reins as elastic rods in your hands, and your arms as extensions of your reins. If your basic arm position is correct, you should be able to draw an imaginary straight line from the pony's bit through the reins to your elbow.

## This is a course with jumps that I rode.

*(Show both the position of the jumps and the course you had to follow. Place a check mark [✔] at the most difficult jump on the course. If you didn't ride a course with jumps, use this space to draw a picture of something special from this show.)*

As I approached the toughest jump, I felt_____

What my pony and I did best today was _____

If I could do any event over again, it would be the _____ class.

I would try to_____

Some things my pony and I need to work on before our next show are_____

_____

**NAME OF SHOW**                                    **WEATHER**

_____

**MY FIRST CLASS WAS**

_____

What my pony and I did best in this class was

_____

We finished_____

Some words that describe the way my pony

behaved as we entered the ring are_____

_____

**A LATER CLASS WAS**

_____

Here's what was running through my head as

I started this class:_____

_____

What my pony and I did best was_____

_____

We finished_____

**MY LAST CLASS WAS**

_____

To psych myself up for this class, I_____

_____

My best moment in this event was_____

_____

My pony and I finished_____

**This is a course with jumps that I rode.**
*(Show both the position of the jumps and the course you had to follow. Place a check mark [✔] at the most difficult jump on the course. If you didn't ride a course with jumps, use this space to draw a picture of something special from this show.)*

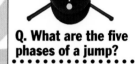

If I were lending my pony to another rider to use in the show, this is the advice I would give her:

_____

If my pony had to explain to another rider how he liked to be ridden, this is what he would say:

_____

# More Memorable Days

Have you ever taken a trail ride with your pony? Have you ever gone swimming with your pony? Ridden on a beach? In the snow? Indoors? These and other riding experiences with your pony might be worth recording as memorable days.

**WHEN AND WHERE:**

✍ _____

_____

_____

_____

_____

**WHEN AND WHERE:**

✍ _____

_____

_____

_____

**WHEN AND WHERE:**

✍ _____

_____

_____

_____

## WHEN AND WHERE:

## WHEN AND WHERE:

## NAME OF SHOW                                        WEATHER

_____

### MY FIRST CLASS WAS

_____

What my pony and I did best was _____

_____

For me, the most challenging part of this

class was _____

_____

My pony and I finished _____

### A LATER CLASS WAS

_____

When my number was called I felt _____

_____

What my pony and I did best was _____

_____

_____

We finished _____

### MY LAST CLASS WAS

_____

My energy level before my last class was

(□ _higher_, □ _lower_) **than at the start of the day.**

I felt _____

My best moment in this event was _____

_____

My pony and I finished _____

## This is a course with jumps that I rode.

*(Show both the position of the jumps and the course you had to follow. Place a check mark [✔] at the most difficult jump on the course. If you didn't ride a course with jumps, use this space to draw a picture of something special from this show.)*

**To calm my pony when we first enter the ring, I always**_____

**If we mess up and have a problem with a jump, I don't panic. Instead, I**_____

_____

**If I were to fall off, I would**_____

**NAME OF SHOW**       **WEATHER**

**MY FIRST CLASS WAS**

What my pony and I did best in this class was

Our biggest problem was_____

My pony and I finished_____

**A LATER CLASS WAS**

If I were the judge, I would say this about my performance in this class:_____

What my pony and I did best was_____

We finished_____

**SHOWS**

If you can, take your pony early to a competition ring to help him get used to it. Be aware of any distractions that make him nervous or tense.

HELPFUL HINT

**MY LAST CLASS WAS**

Whenever I go into this class, my instructor always reminds me to_____

My best moment in this class was_____

My pony and I finished_____

**This is a course with jumps that I rode.**

*(Show both the position of the jumps and the course you had to follow. Place a check mark [✔] at the most difficult jump on the course. If you didn't ride a course with jumps, use this space to draw a picture of something special from this show.)*

**If my pony could talk, this is what he would have been telling me during my best class today:**

_____

_____

_____

## NAME OF SHOW                    WEATHER

_____

## MY FIRST CLASS WAS

_____

What my pony and I did best in this class was

_____

Some words that describe my pony's mood or

feelings before this class are:_____

_____

My pony and I finished_____

## SHOW

Before riding any competition course in a show, learn the course by studying its diagram, watching the riders ahead of you, and practicing in the practice ring. Count your pony's strides between jumps, and make check points for yourself midway between each jump. That way, in competition, you can adjust your pony's stride if it is ahead or behind the checkpoint. Also, note the course's terrain and visualize yourself riding the course well.

HELPFUL HINT

## A LATER CLASS WAS

_____

My goal for this class was to_____

_____

What my pony and I did best was_____

_____

_____

We finished_____

## MY LAST CLASS WAS

_____

Going into this event, my pony told me he felt

_____

Here's how he told me:_____

_____

My best moment in this event was_____

_____

My pony and I finished_____

## The Ultimate Jump

*(At many shows, courses include some beautiful jumps that have been carefully constructed by the course designer. Use the space below to draw a jump that you think would be both beautiful and challenging. Include some of the many items normally used to construct jumps such as rails, bushes, and barrels, but remember: keep it safe and don't forget the ground line.)*

# And Even More Memorable Days

Use this section to write about some of your other pony-related activities. These might include a great ride you had with your riding buddies, a picnic, a camp out with your pony. Have you gone as a spectator to any horse shows lately? Have you had an interesting Pony Club meeting? Have you purchased any new clothing or equipment? Has anything interesting happened at your stable? Use this space to write about such memorable events.

**WHEN AND WHERE:**

**WHEN AND WHERE:**

**WHEN AND WHERE:**

**WHEN AND WHERE:**

✎ _____

_____

_____

_____

_____

**WHEN AND WHERE:**

✎ _____

_____

_____

_____

_____

**NAME OF SHOW**                                    **WEATHER**

_____

**MY FIRST CLASS WAS**

_____

What my pony and I did best in this class was

_____

We finished_____

Warming up, I knew it was going to be a *(❏ good,*

*❏ bad, ❏ OK)* **class because**_____

_____

**A LATER CLASS WAS**

_____

For me, the most challenging part of this

class was _____

_____

What my pony and I did best was_____

_____

We finished _____

**MY LAST CLASS WAS**

_____

My best advice for anyone entering this class

would be_____

_____

My best moment in this event was_____

_____

My pony and I finished_____

**This is a course with jumps that I rode.**
*(Show both the position of the jumps and the course you had to follow. Place a check mark [✔] at the most difficult jump on the course. If you didn't ride a course with jumps, use this space to draw a picture of something special from this show.)*

If a show is more than one day long, I sometimes stay overnight *(where)*_____

_____ . My favorite part of these overnights is_____

_____ . At the show itself, my idea of a great lunch is

_____ and for a snack I can't resist_____.

Sometimes I buy souvenirs at shows. If I had lots of money to spend at a souvenir stand I

would buy_____.

## NAME OF SHOW

## WEATHER

_____

## MY FIRST CLASS WAS

_____

**What my pony and I did best in this class was**

_____

**Compared to our performance in earlier shows, this class went** (❑ *well,* ❑ *about the same,* ❑ *poorly)* **for us because**_____

_____

**We finished**_____

## A LATER CLASS WAS

_____

**When my number was called, I felt**_____

_____

**What my pony and I did best was**_____

_____

**We finished**_____

## MY LAST CLASS WAS

_____

**My pony's advice to other ponies competing in this class would be**_____

_____

**My best moment in this event was**_____

_____

**My pony and I finished**_____

**Q. Who was Pegasus?**

A. The winged, flying horse from Greek mythology. He was tamed by the hero Bellerophon using a golden bridle from the goddess Athena. Later, Bellerophon tried to ride Pegasus to heaven, but the great horse threw him off. Today, the constellation Pegasus can be seen in the northern sky, especially in winter.

**This is a course with jumps that I rode.**
*(Show both the position of the jumps and the course you had to follow. Place a check mark [✔] at the most difficult jump on the course. If you didn't ride a course with jumps, use this space to draw a picture of something special from this show.)*

**If I were an equestrian writer, I would use these words to describe the following riding sensations:**

1. The smell of my pony: _____

2. How it feels when I canter my pony: _____

3. How it feels to take a jump: _____

4. How it feels when everything goes right in a class: _____

## NAME OF SHOW                    WEATHER

_____

## MY FIRST CLASS WAS

_____

What my pony and I did best in this class was

_____

If I could have played a song while I competed

in this class it would have been_____

_____because

_____

## A LATER CLASS WAS

_____

Compared to earlier in the season, my pony

and I are better at this class now. Here's how:

_____

What my pony and I did best was_____

_____

We finished_____

## POISE

**HELPFUL HINT**

When leaving a competition ring, no matter how well or poorly you have done, be a good sport. Remember: nobody likes a sore loser or a stuck-up winner.

## MY LAST CLASS WAS

_____

The key to doing well in this class is_____

_____

My best moment in this event was_____

_____

My pony and I finished_____

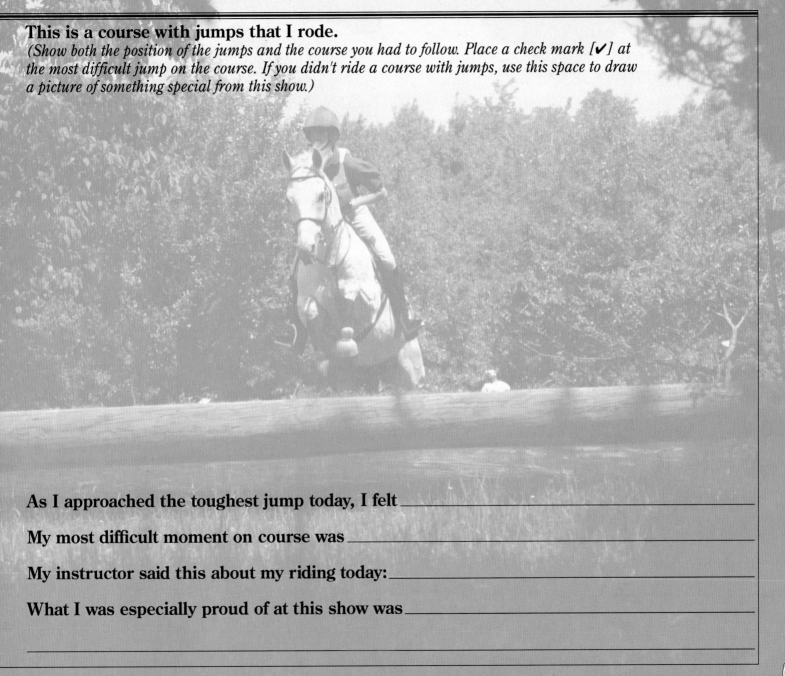

**This is a course with jumps that I rode.**
*(Show both the position of the jumps and the course you had to follow. Place a check mark [✔] at the most difficult jump on the course. If you didn't ride a course with jumps, use this space to draw a picture of something special from this show.)*

As I approached the toughest jump today, I felt _____

My most difficult moment on course was _____

My instructor said this about my riding today: _____

What I was especially proud of at this show was _____

_____

# My Best Show

My best show of the season was

_____

Here's why: _____

_____

_____

Some words that describe the way I felt after

completing that show are _____

_____

I improved as a pony rider this year in the

following ways: _____

_____

_____

My pony and I still need to improve on these

things: _____

_____

_____

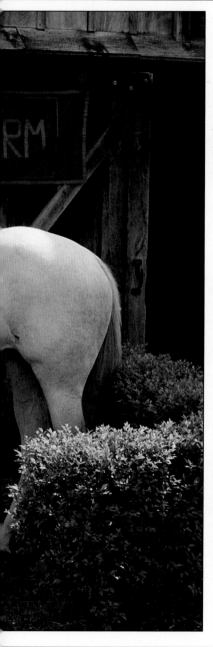

# Other Events for Me and My Pony

*(Use these spaces to tell about any other kinds of events in which you might have participated this season such as Pony Club rallies, gymkhanas, 4H competitions, and so on.)*

# Next Year's Wish List

If I could have anything next season for my pony and

me, it would be these things:_____

_____

_____

If I could go anywhere with my pony, it would be to

_____

because_____

_____

## MY RIDING COLLECTION

The five most favorite things in my riding collection
are *(list special items such as horse statues, posters, even autographs)*:

1. _____

2. _____

3. _____

4. _____

5. _____

The most special is_____

because_____

# My Favorite Books and Films About Horses and Ponies

My favorite books about horses or ponies are

_____

_____

My favorite instructional books on riding are

_____

My favorite movies about horses or ponies

are_____

In _____ I like the part when

_____

_____

| READING LIST | FILM LIST |
| --- | --- |
| **How many of these books have you read?** | **How many of these films have you seen?** |
| ❑ Black Beauty | ❑ National Velvet |
| ❑ Justin Morgan Had a Horse | ❑ Phar Lap |
| ❑ My Friend Flicka | ❑ My Friend Flicka |
| ❑ The Red Pony | ❑ The Red Pony |
| ❑ Misty of Chincoteague | ❑ The Black Stallion |
| ❑ Stormy, Misty's Foal | ❑ Man from Snowy River |
| ❑ The Horse-Tamer | ❑ Wild Hearts Can't Be Broken |
| ❑ The Horse in the Attic | ❑ _____ |
| ❑ The Island Stallion Races | ❑ _____ |
| ❑ _____ | ❑ _____ |

# My Own Personal Riding Tips and Tricks

I know a lot about riding. Here are some tips and tricks that have made me a better rider:

When bridling my pony, I get him to open his mouth by_____

When saddling a pony, I always check _____

I get my pony to do a nice walk by_____

When riding my pony at a trot, I know I'm on the correct diagonal when_____

_____

I ask my pony to canter by_____

I know I am on the correct lead when _____

The position I use for galloping is_____

When jumping my pony, I always remind myself to_____

The most important riding tips I tell myself over and over are_____

_____

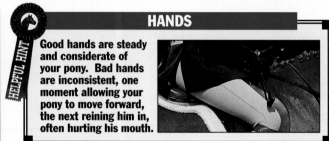

**HANDS**

HELPFUL HINT

Good hands are steady and considerate of your pony. Bad hands are inconsistent, one moment allowing your pony to move forward, the next reining him in, often hurting his mouth.

## HOLDING THE REINS

When holding the reins, keep your fingers closed and pinch the reins firmly between your thumb and forefinger. That way, if your pony stumbles or jerks his head, you won't lose control of the reins.

# Clippings and Stuff from My Riding Season

Use this section to save any pictures, ticket stubs, newspaper clippings, or other mementos from your riding year. See how much you can put on these pages so they look like a collage.

15. CHILDREN'S HUNTER PONY UNDER SADDLE. Walk, trot, canter.
    Light contact with pony's mouth required. Martingales not
    permitted.
16. CHILDREN'S HUNTER PONY.
17. CHILDREN'S HUNTER PONY.
    CHILDREN'S HUNTER PONY CHAMPIONSHIP. To be awarded to two
    of the four ponies scoring the most points in Classes 16-
    ___ ___tition, only these will receive full points for
    ___ ___ ___ Reserve.                    Walk, trot, canter.
                                            ___ingales

# My Three Favorite Riders

*(an Olympic champion, favorite instructor, or even a good friend)*:

1._____

2._____

3._____

I like_____ best

because_____

_____

_____

# My Season's Highlight

**Of all the things that happened this riding**

**season, what I'll always remember is**_____

_____

_____

_____

_____

_____

## IMPORTANT PEOPLE AND PHONE NUMBERS

| | | |
|---|---|---|
| **My Stable Manager**_____ ☎ |  |  |
| **My Instructor**_____ ☎ |  |  |
| **My Veterinarian** _____ ☎ |  |  |
| **My Farrier**_____ ☎ |  |  |
| **Dad at work/home** ☎ ____ ☎ |  |  |
| **Mom at work/home** ☎ ___ ☎ |  |  |
| **My Riding Buddies** _____ ☎ |  |  |
| _____ ☎ |  |  |
| _____ ☎ |  |  |
| **Fire**_____ ☎ |  |  |
| **Police**_____ ☎ |  |  |

## CREDITS

WRITING AND PHOTOGRAPHY: **Tom Ettinger, Bill Jaspersohn**
DESIGN: **Joseph Lee (HOPKINS/BAUMANN)**

THE AUTHORS WISH TO THANK THE FOLLOWING FOR THEIR HELP:
Jeanie Clarke; Linda and Stacey Johnston, Brookwood Farm, Montpelier, VT; Janet Larson; Barbara Lindsay, Wayside Farm, Bedford, NY; Bonnie Loomis-Cunniffe, Whipstick Farm, South Salem, NY; Allison Thurston-Palermo.

AND A VERY SPECIAL THANKS TO: Emily Harris and Fred; Angela McLaughlin and Poppy; Alex Palermo and Possum; Bailey Spaulding and Frog; Abigail Spaulding and Chaucer.